ADELE

FOR BEGINNING PIANO SOLO

2 All I Ask

6 Chasing Pavements

10 Hello

19 Remedy

14 Rolling in the Deep

22 Set Fire to the Rain

27 Skyfall

38 Someone Like You

30 Turning Tables

34 When We Were Young

Cover photo © Pictorial Press Ltd / Alamy

ISBN 978-1-4950-5883-7

HAL•LEONARD® CORPORATION

7777 W. Bluemound Rd. P.O. Box 13819 Milwaukee, WI 53213

For all works contained herein:
Unauthorized copying, arranging, adapting, recording, Internet posting, public performance or other distribution of the printed music in this publication is an infringement of copyright. Infringers are liable under the law.

Visit Hal Leonard Online at
www.halleonard.com

T0018992

ALL I ASK

Words and Music by ADELE ADKINS,
PHILIP LAWRENCE, BRUNO MARS
and CHRIS BROWN

Copyright © 2015 MELTED STONE PUBLISHING LTD., ZZR MUSIC LLC, BMG RIGHTS MANAGEMENT (US) LLC, MARS FORCE MUSIC,
WB MUSIC CORP., THOU ART THE HUNGER, WESTSIDE INDEPENDENT MUSIC PUBLISHING LLC and LATE 80'S MUSIC
This arrangement Copyright © 2016 MELTED STONE PUBLISHING LTD., ZZR MUSIC LLC, BMG RIGHTS MANAGEMENT (US) LLC,
MARS FORCE MUSIC, WB MUSIC CORP., THOU ART THE HUNGER, WESTSIDE INDEPENDENT MUSIC PUBLISHING LLC and LATE 80'S MUSIC
All Rights for MELTED STONE PUBLISHING LTD. in the U.S. and Canada Administered by UNIVERSAL - SONGS OF POLYGRAM INTERNATIONAL, INC.
All Rights for ZZR MUSIC LLC Administered by UNIVERSAL MUSIC CORP.
All Rights for MARS FORCE MUSIC Administered by BMG RIGHTS MANAGEMENT (US) LLC
All Rights for THOU ART THE HUNGER Administered by WB MUSIC CORP.
All Rights for THOU ART THE HUNGER and LATE 80'S MUSIC Administered by WESTSIDE INDEPENDENT MUSIC PUBLISHING LLC
All Rights Reserved Used by Permission

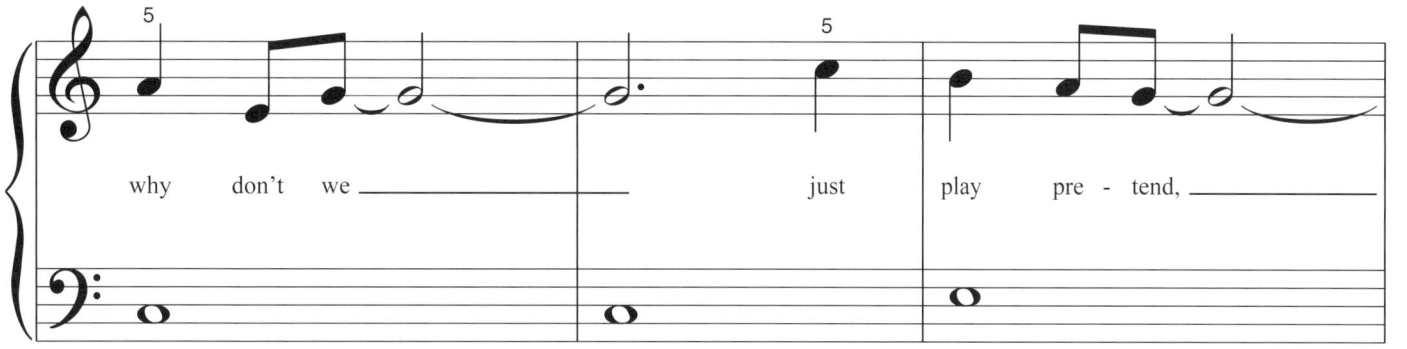
why don't we
just play pre - tend,

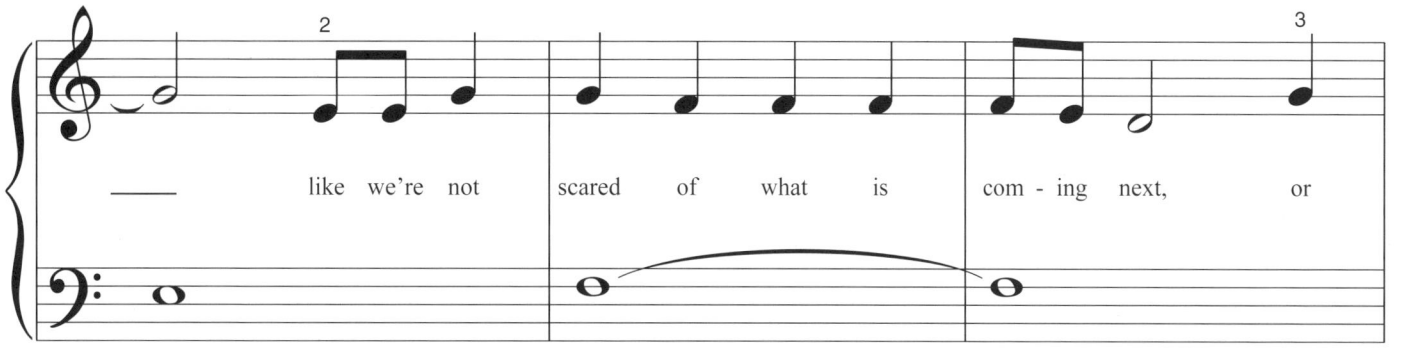
like we're not scared of what is com - ing next, or

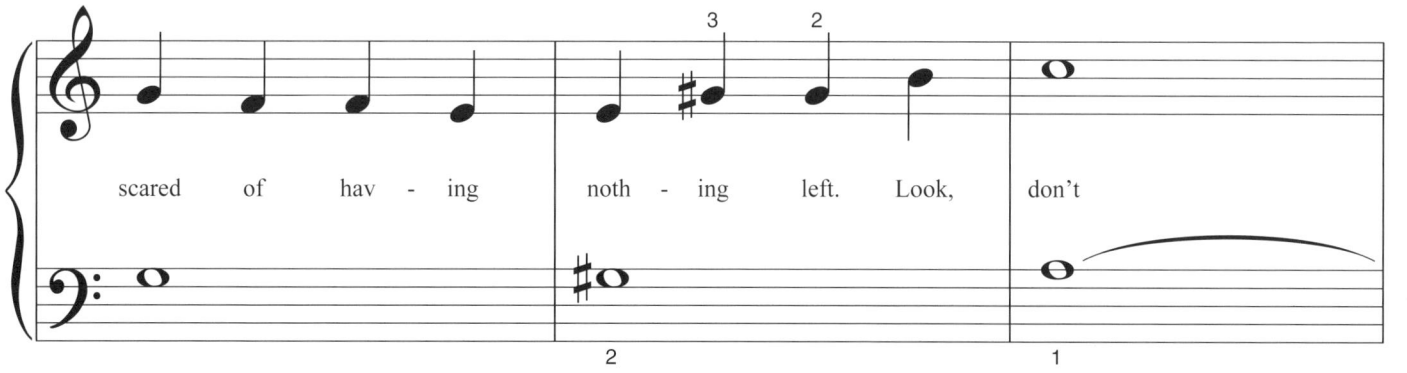
scared of hav - ing noth - ing left. Look, don't

get me wrong, I know there is no to - mor -

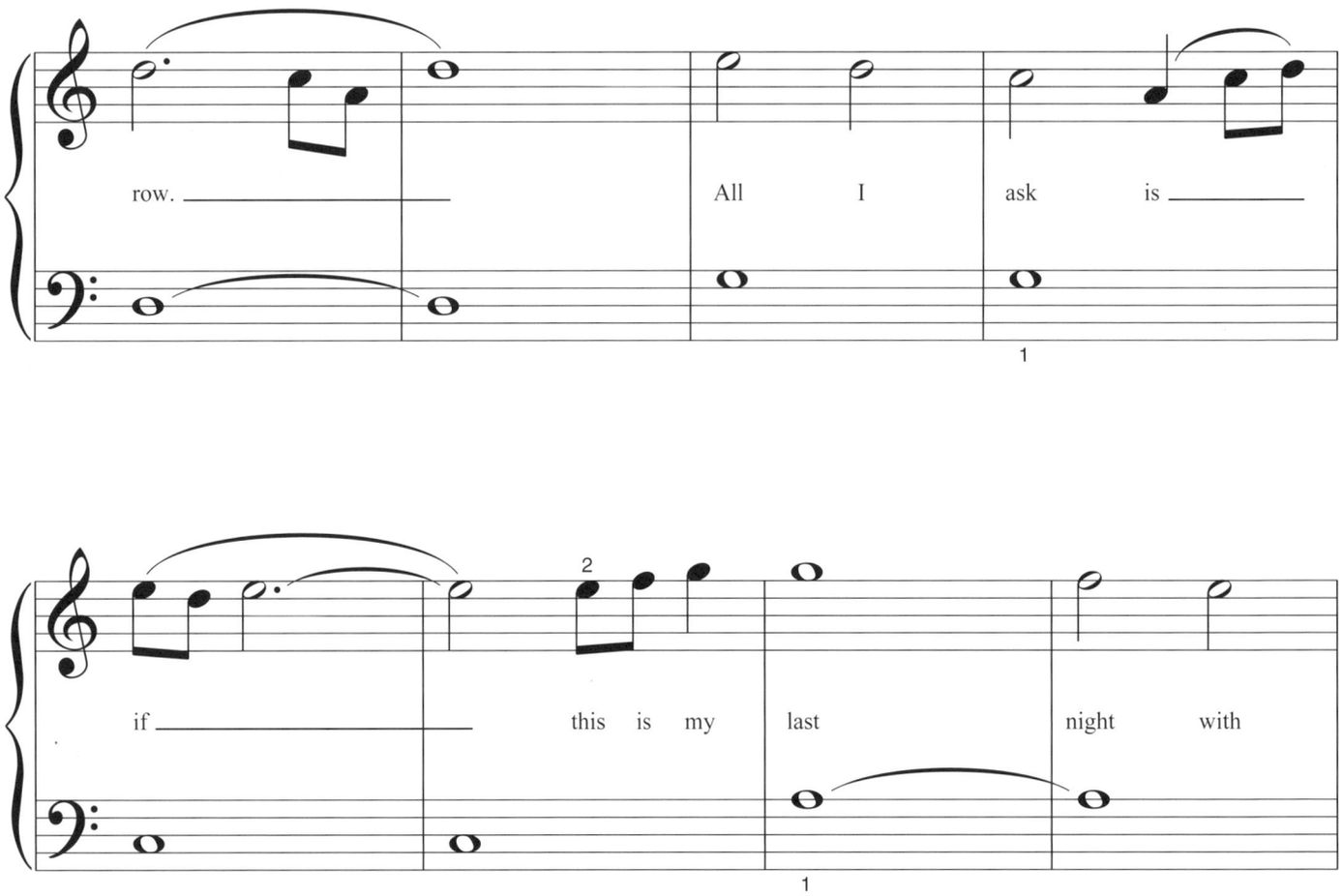
row.
All I ask is
1
if
2
this is my last night with
1

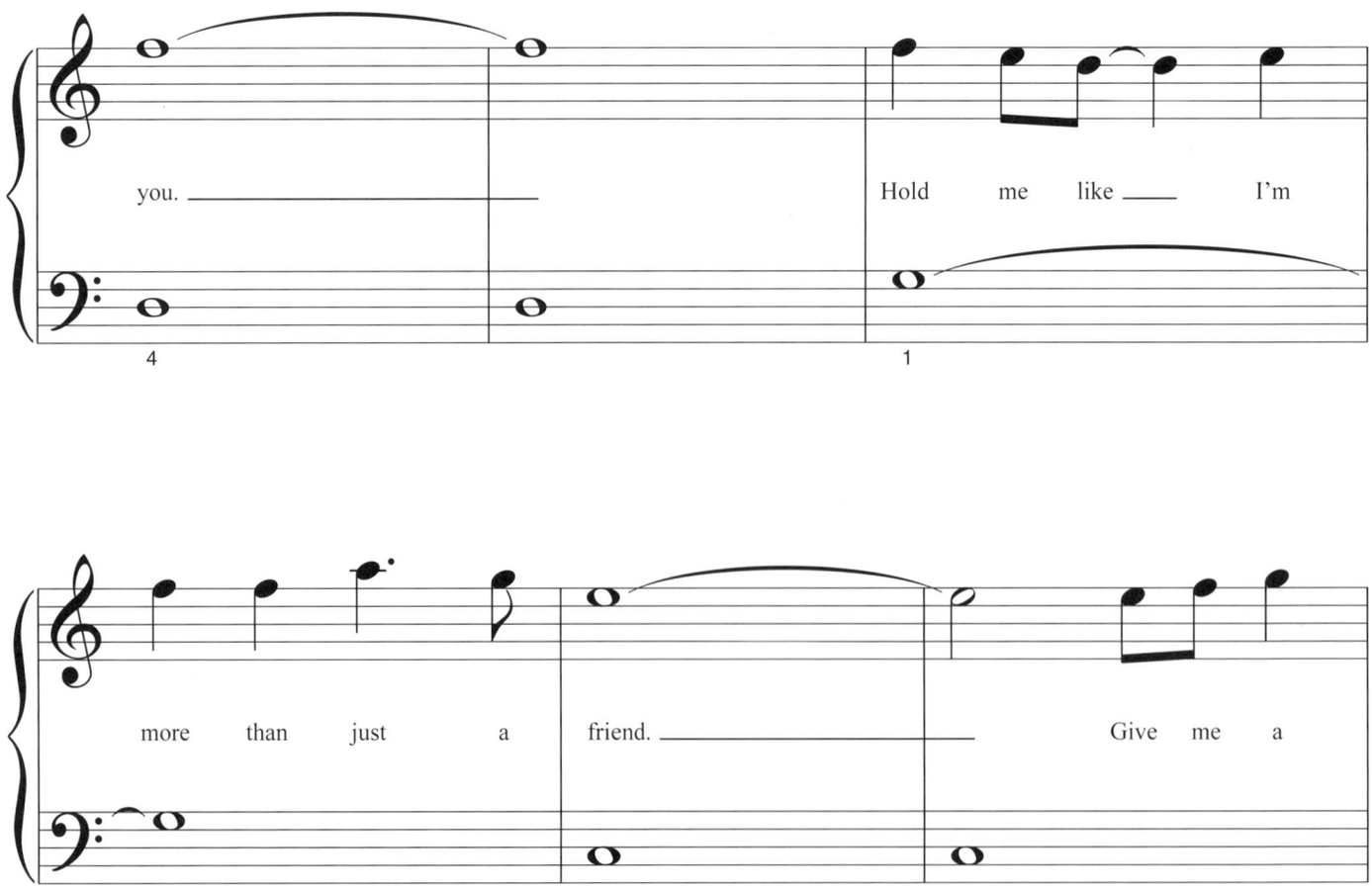
you.
Hold me like I'm
4
1
more than just a friend.
Give me a

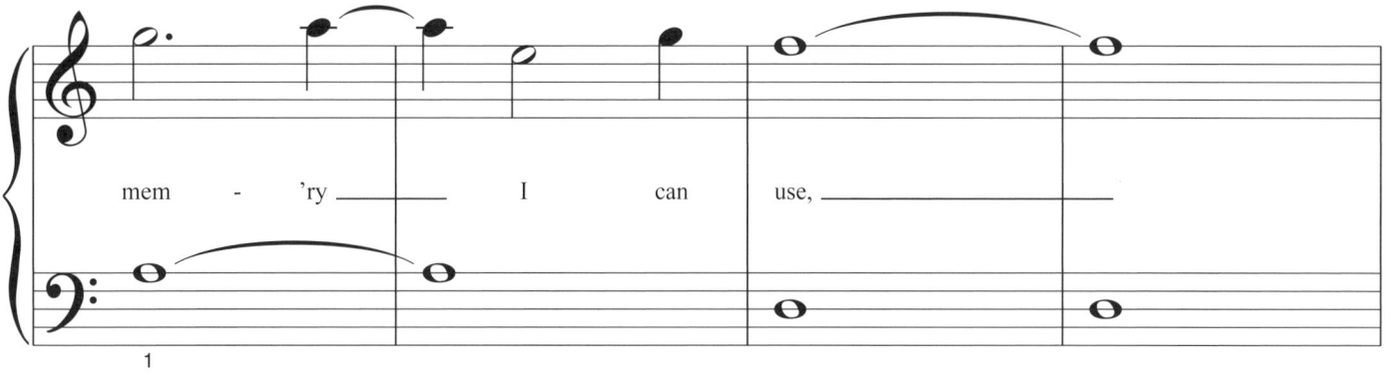
mem - 'ry I can use,
1

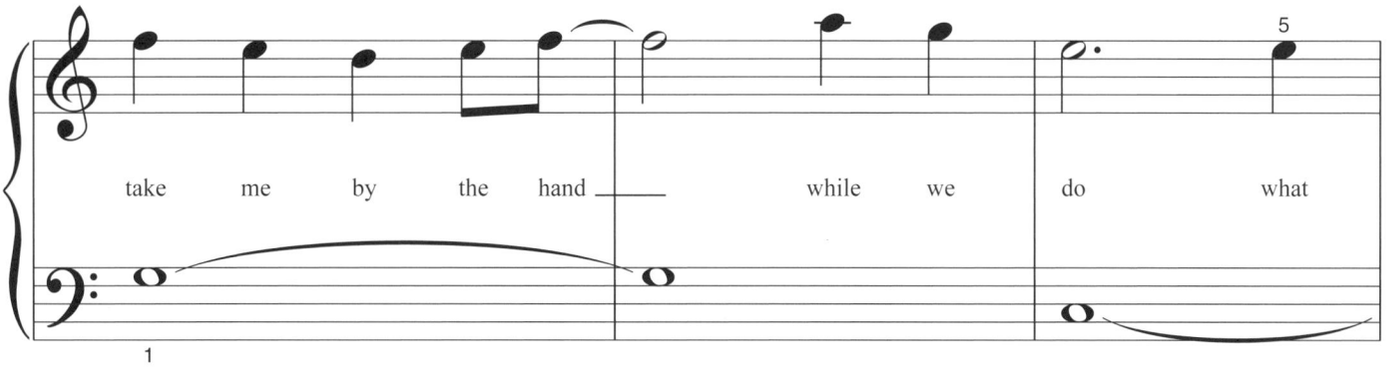
5
take me by the hand while we do what
1

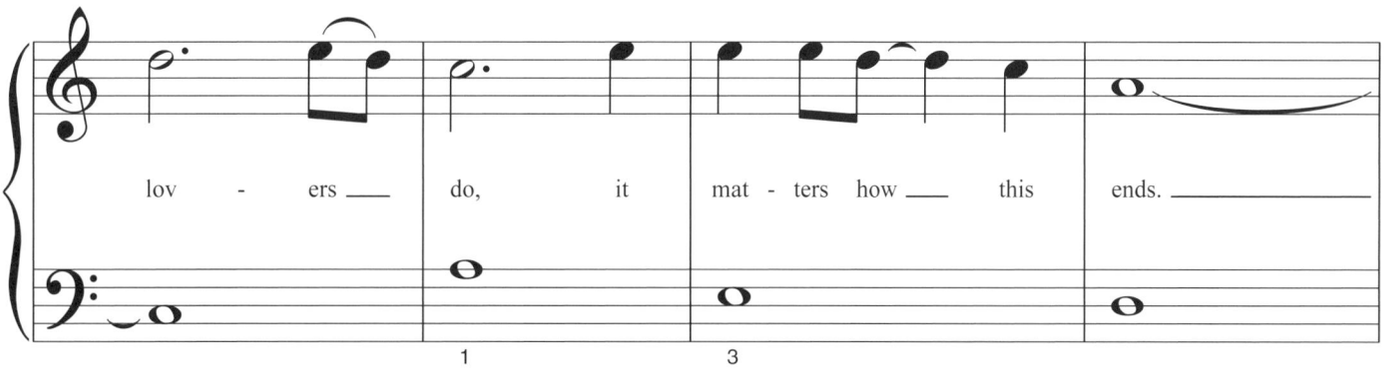
lov - ers do, it mat - ters how this ends.
1
3

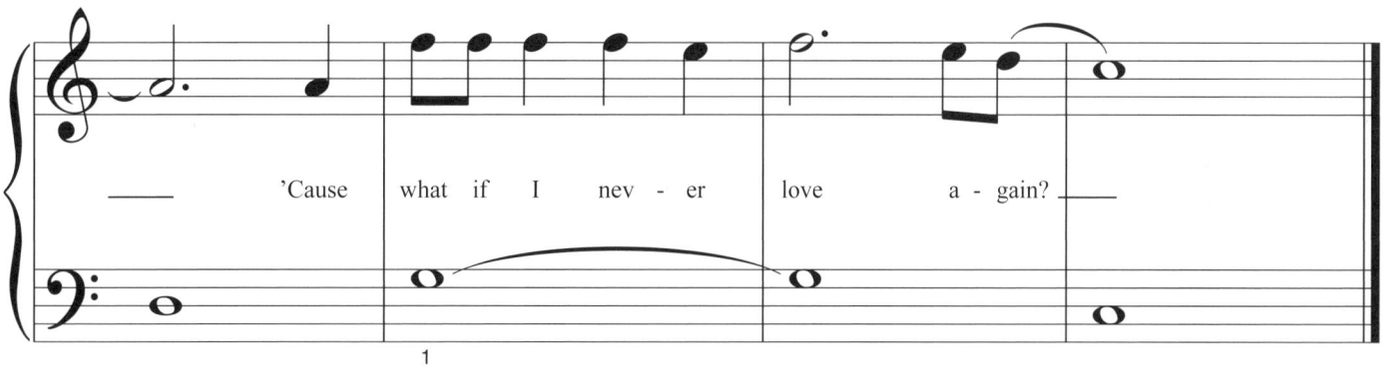
'Cause what if I nev - er love a - gain?
1

CHASING PAVEMENTS

Words and Music by ADELE ADKINS
and FRANCIS EG WHITE

Copyright © 2008 MELTED STONE PUBLISHING LTD. and UNIVERSAL MUSIC PUBLISHING LTD.
This arrangement Copyright © 2016 MELTED STONE PUBLISHING LTD. and UNIVERSAL MUSIC PUBLISHING LTD.
All Rights in the U.S. and Canada Controlled and Administered by UNIVERSAL - SONGS OF POLYGRAM INTERNATIONAL, INC.
All Rights Reserved Used by Permission

nev - er say e - nough, 'cause it was not said to you, and that's ex -

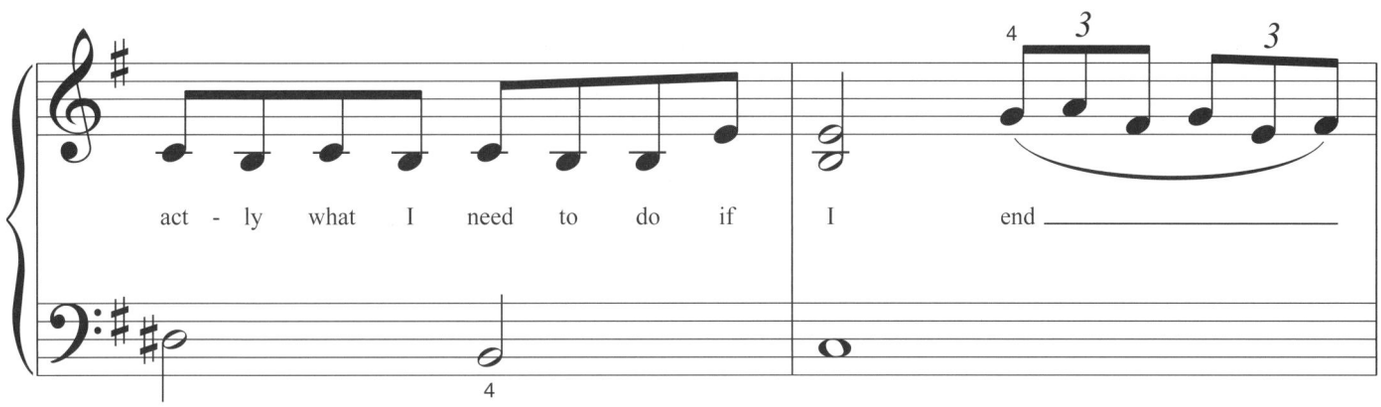
act - ly what I need to do if I end

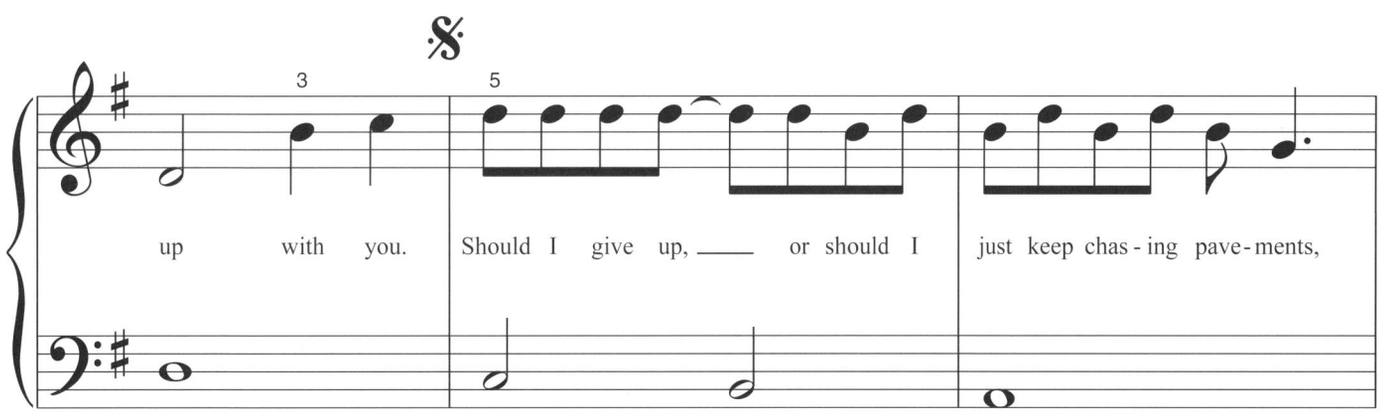
up with you. Should I give up, or should I just keep chas - ing pave - ments,

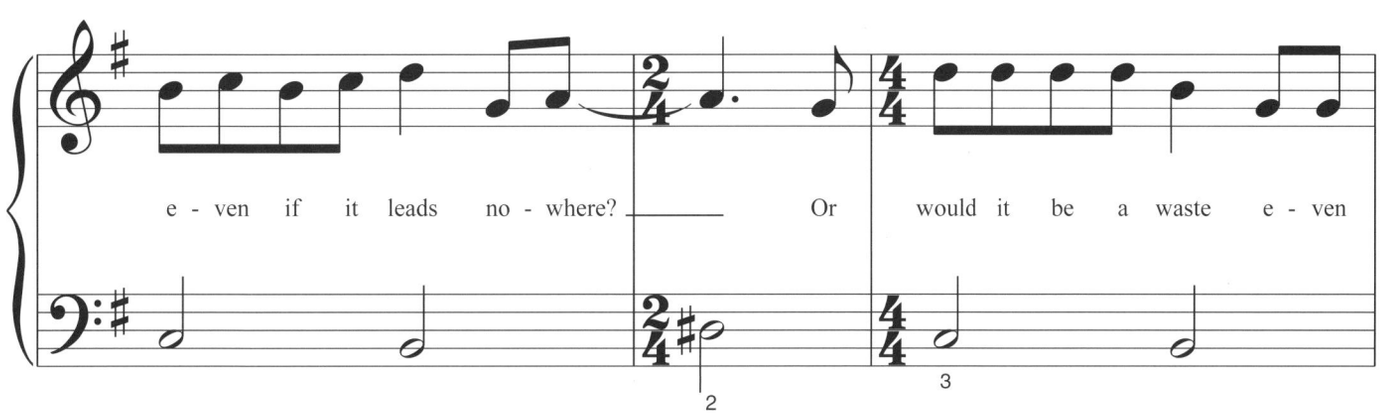
e - ven if it leads no - where? Or would it be a waste e - ven

4 2 3
if I knew my place? Should I leave it there? Should I give up, or should I

To Coda
5 2
just keep chas - ing pave - ments, e - ven if it leads no - where?
5

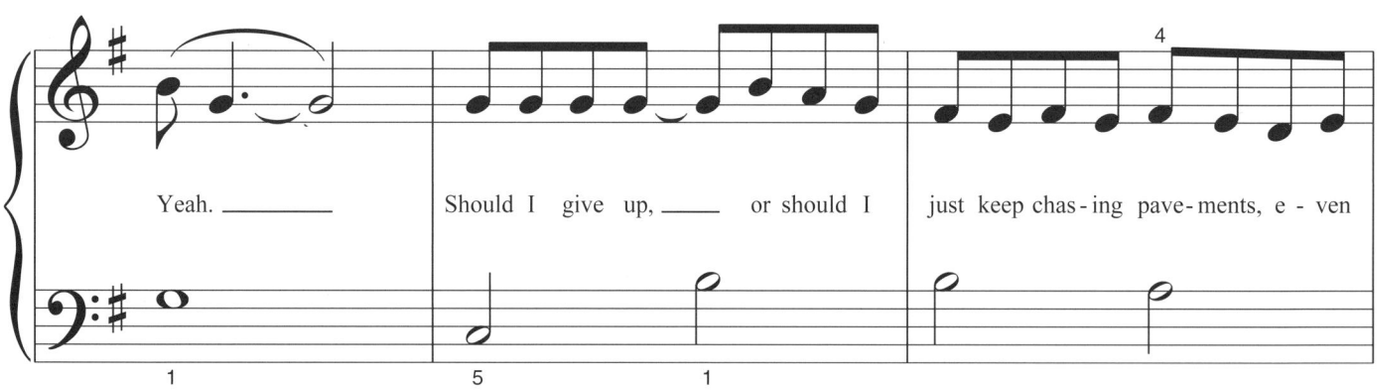
4
Yeah. Should I give up, or should I just keep chas - ing pave - ments, e - ven
1 5 1

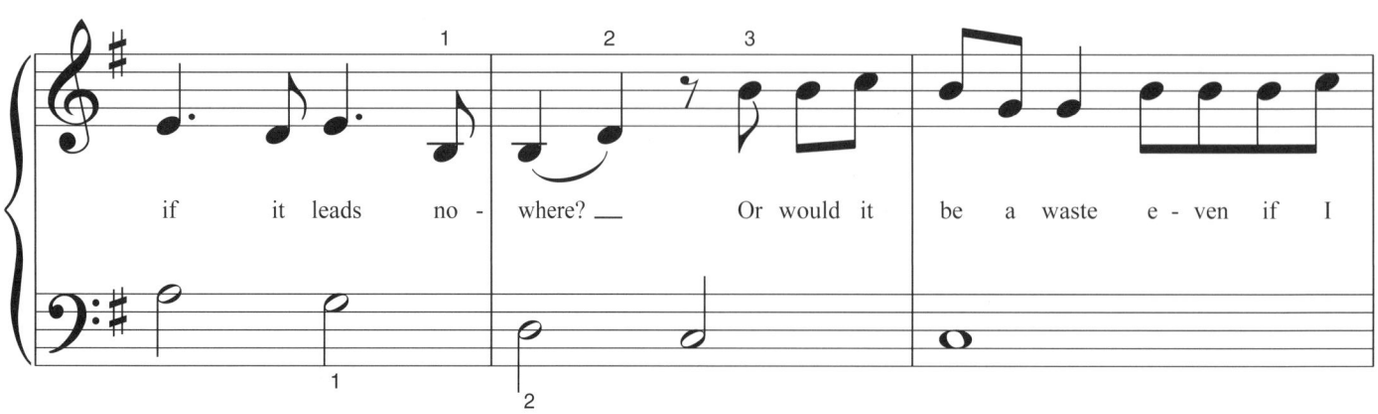
1 2 3
if it leads no - where? Or would it be a waste e - ven if I
1 2

D.S. al Coda

CODA

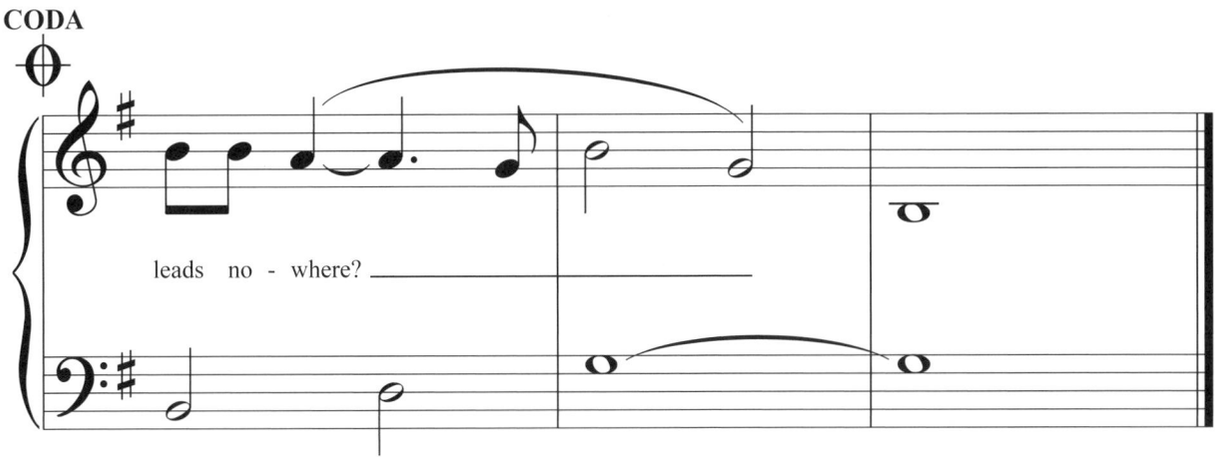

HELLO

Words and Music by ADELE ADKINS
and GREG KURSTIN

Copyright © 2015 MELTED STONE PUBLISHING LTD., EMI APRIL MUSIC INC. and KURSTIN MUSIC
This arrangement Copyright © 2016 MELTED STONE PUBLISHING LTD., EMI APRIL MUSIC INC. and KURSTIN MUSIC
All Rights for MELTED STONE PUBLISHING LTD. in the U.S. and Canada Administered by UNIVERSAL - SONGS OF POLYGRAM INTERNATIONAL, INC.
All Rights for EMI APRIL MUSIC INC. and KURSTIN MUSIC Administered by SONY/ATV MUSIC PUBLISHING LLC, 424 Church Street, Suite 1200, Nashville, TN 37219
All Rights Reserved Used by Permission

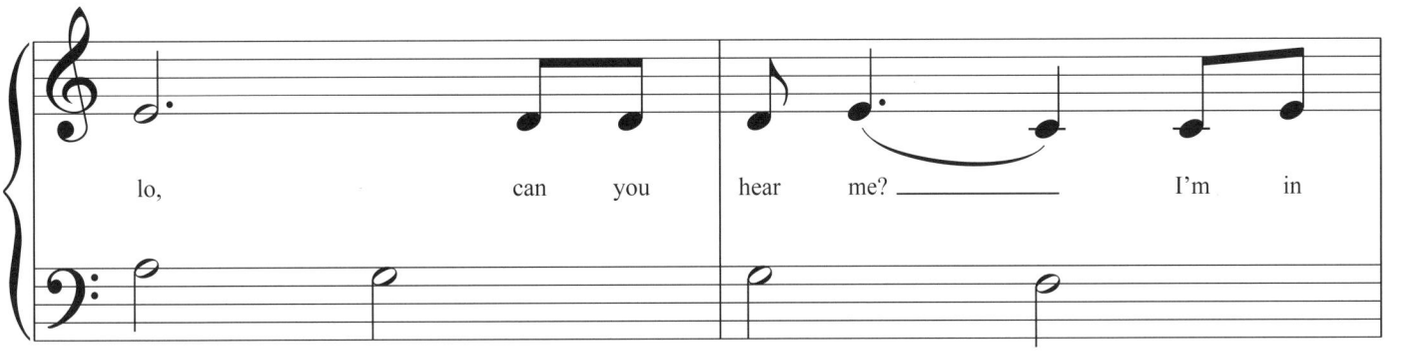
lo, can you hear me? I'm in

Cal - i - for - nia dream - ing a - bout who we used to be when we were

young - er and free. I've for -

got - ten how it felt be - fore the world fell at our feet. There's such a

dif - f'rence be - tween ___ us, ___ and a mil - li - on ___ miles. ___

1
___ Hel - lo from the oth - er side. ___ I

1
must have called a thou - sand times ___ to tell you ___

4
___ I'm sor - ry for ev - 'ry - thing that I've done, ___ but when I

3
4
call you nev - er seem to be home. Hel - lo from the out - side.

1
At least I can say that I've tried to tell you

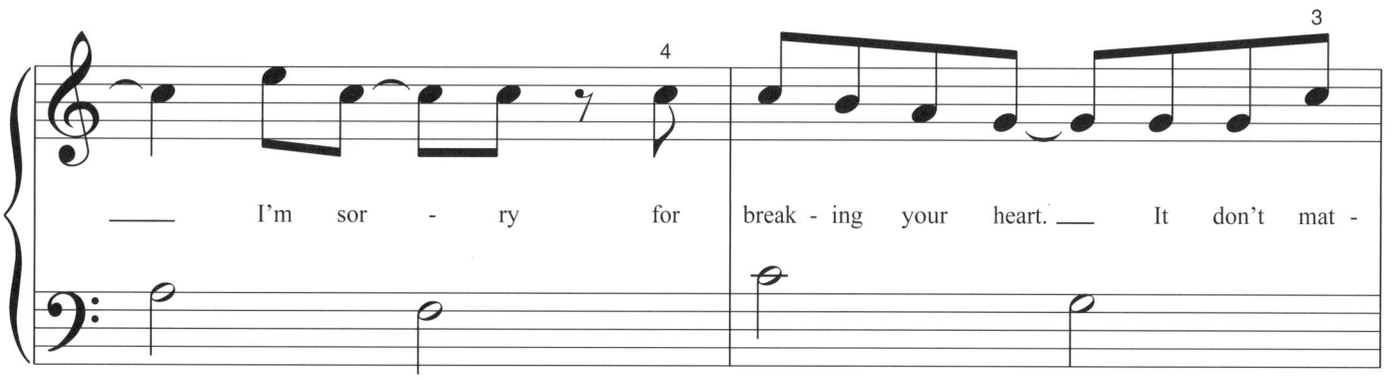
4
3
I'm sor - ry for break - ing your heart. It don't mat -

5
ter: it clear - ly does - n't tear you a - part an - y - more.

ROLLING IN THE DEEP

Words and Music by ADELE ADKINS
and PAUL EPWORTH

Copyright © 2010, 2011 MELTED STONE PUBLISHING LTD. and EMI MUSIC PUBLISHING LTD.
This arrangement Copyright © 2016 MELTED STONE PUBLISHING LTD. and EMI MUSIC PUBLISHING LTD.
All Rights for MELTED STONE PUBLISHING LTD. in the U.S. and Canada Controlled and Administered by UNIVERSAL - SONGS OF POLYGRAM INTERNATIONAL, INC.
All Rights for EMI MUSIC PUBLISHING LTD. Administered by SONY/ATV MUSIC PUBLISHING LLC, 424 Church Street, Suite 1200, Nashville, TN 37219
All Rights Reserved Used by Permission

don't un - der - es - ti - mate the things that I will do.
I've heard ____ one on you. I'm gonna make your head burn.

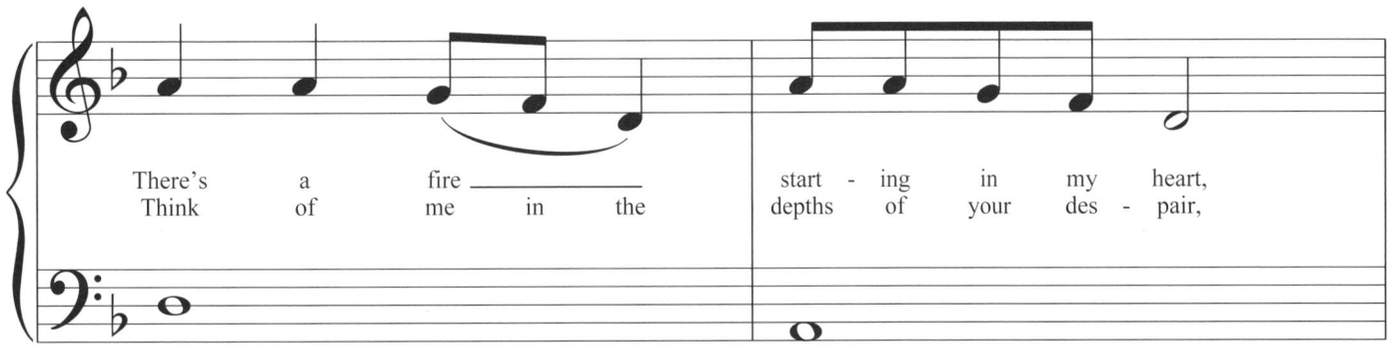
There's a fire ____ start - ing in my heart,
Think of me in the depths of your des - pair,

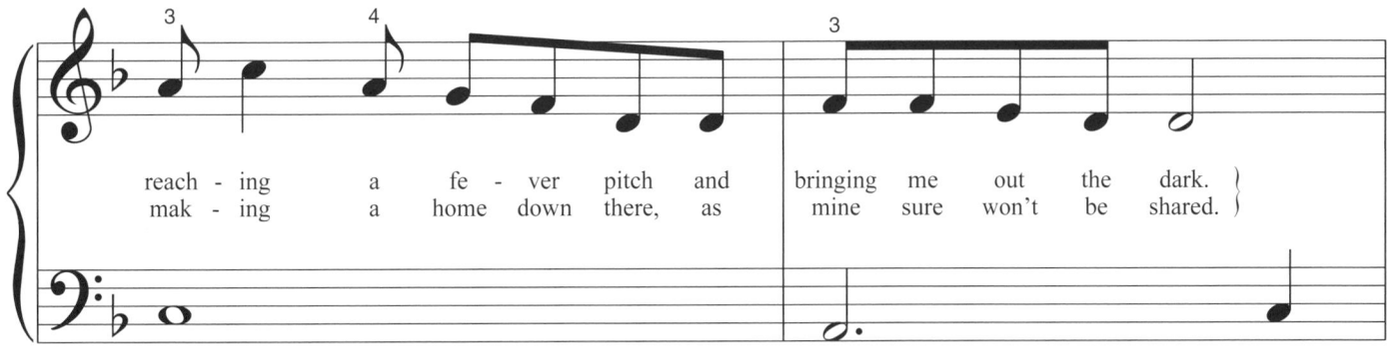
reach - ing a fe - ver pitch and bringing me out the dark.
mak - ing a home down there, as mine sure won't be shared.

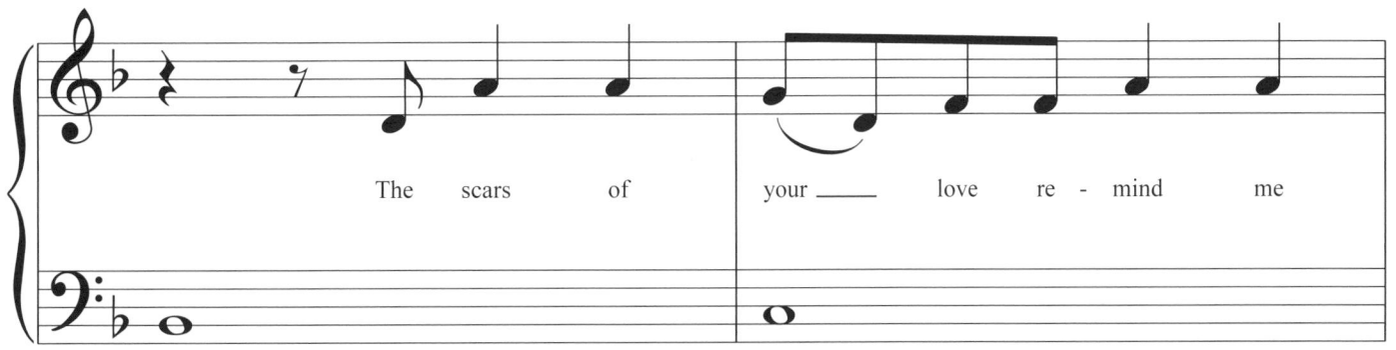
The scars of your ____ love re - mind me

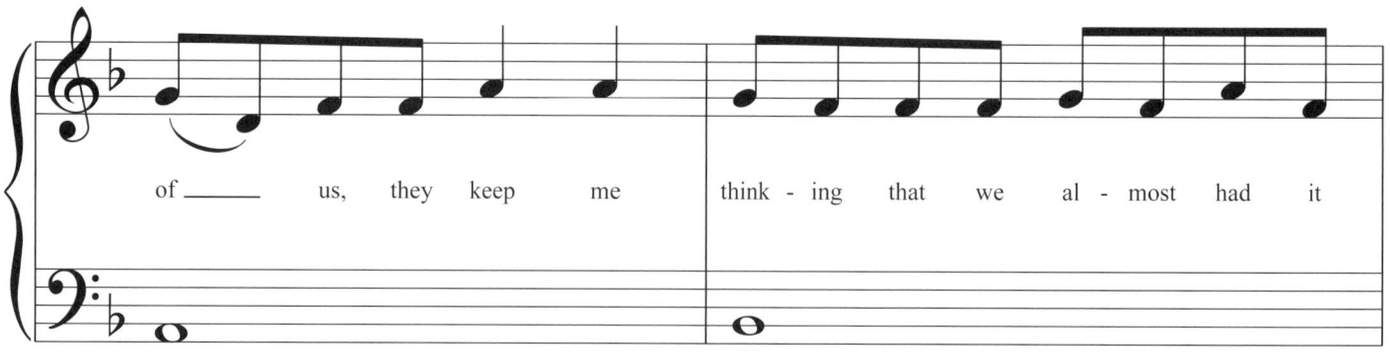
of us, they keep me
think - ing that we al - most had it

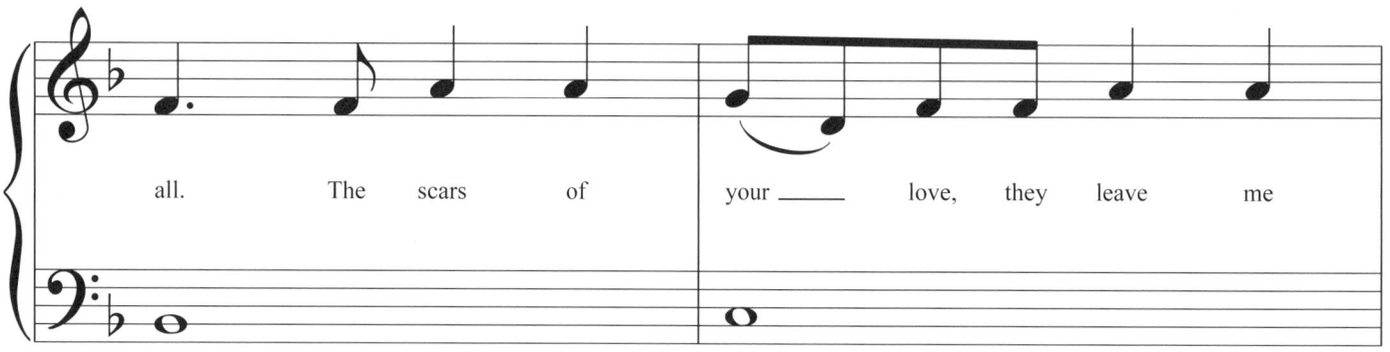
all. The scars of
your love, they leave me

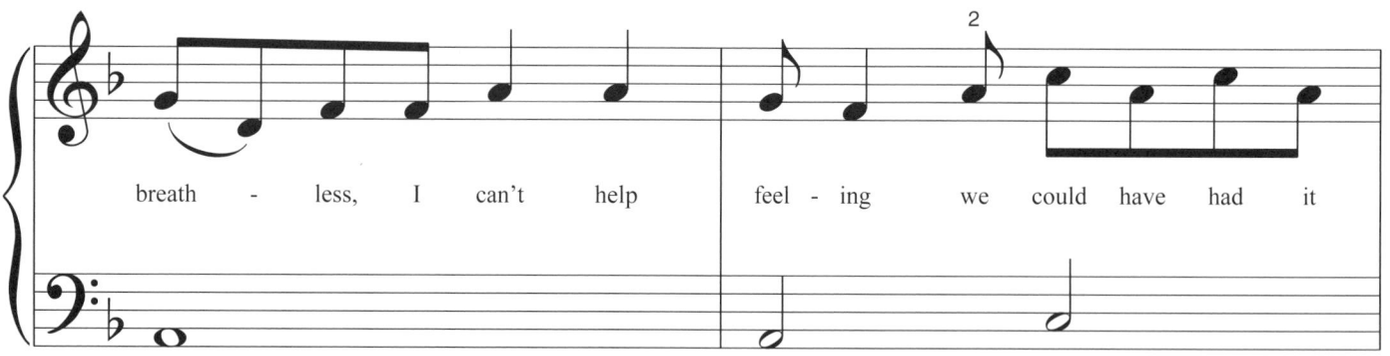
breath - less, I can't help
2
feel - ing we could have had it

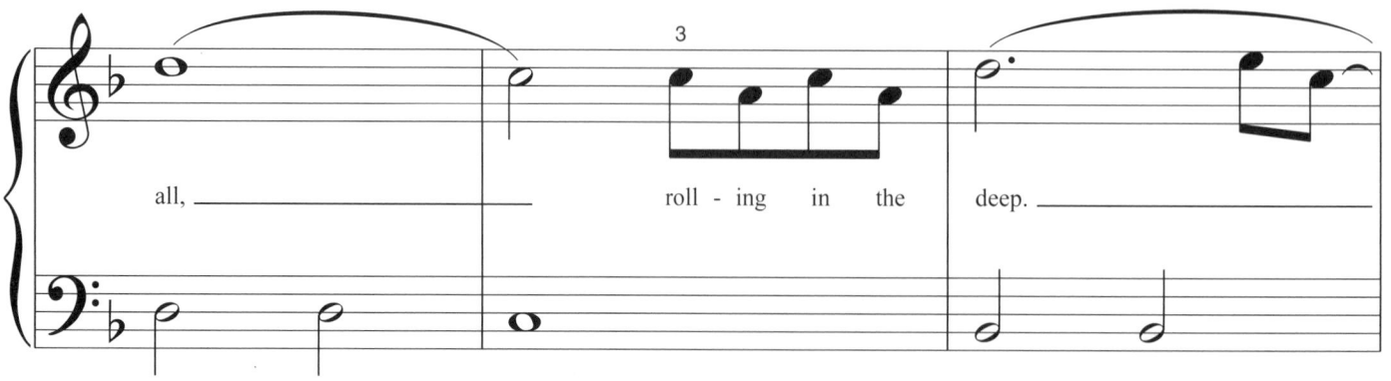
all,
3
roll - ing in the
deep.

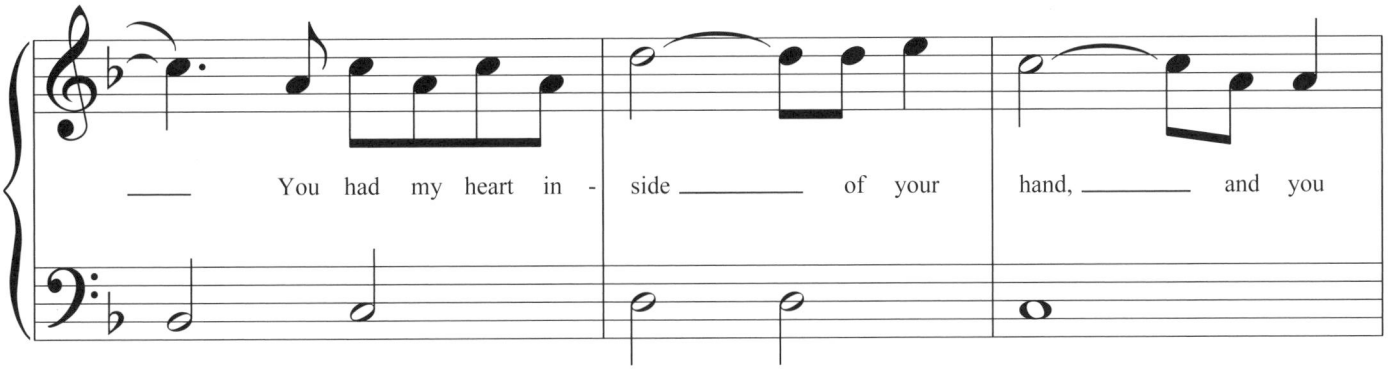
You had my heart in - side of your hand, and you

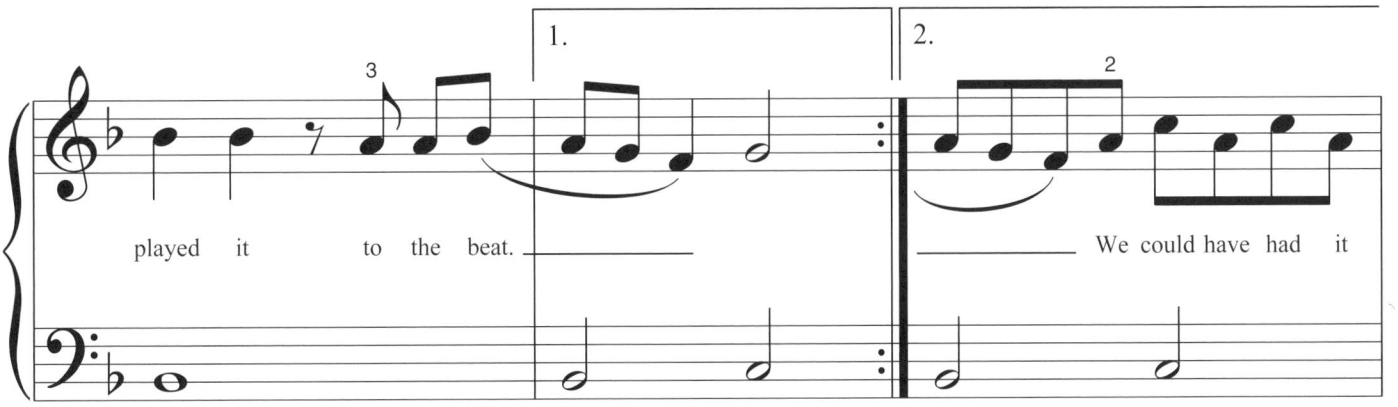
1.
2.
3
2
played it to the beat.
We could have had it

3
all.
Roll - ing in the deep.

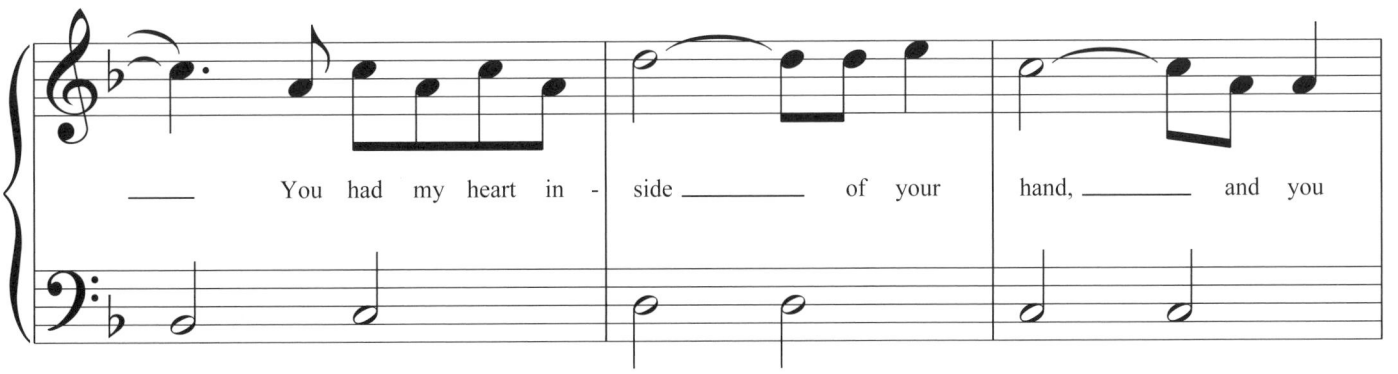
You had my heart in - side of your hand, and you

3
2
played it to the beat. We could have had it all.

3
Roll - ing in the deep. You had my heart in -

3
side of your hand, but you played

4
it, you played it, you played it, you played it to the beat.

REMEDY

Words and Music by ADELE ADKINS
and RYAN TEDDER

Copyright © 2015 MELTED STONE PUBLISHING LTD. and WRITE ME A SONG PUBLISHING
This arrangement Copyright © 2016 MELTED STONE PUBLISHING LTD. and WRITE ME A SONG PUBLISHING
All Rights for MELTED STONE PUBLISHING LTD. in the U.S. and Canada Administered by UNIVERSAL - SONGS OF POLYGRAM INTERNATIONAL, INC.
All Rights for WRITE ME A SONG PUBLISHING Administered Worldwide by KOBALT MUSIC GROUP LTD.
All Rights Reserved Used by Permission

saw, my heart it came to life. This ain't

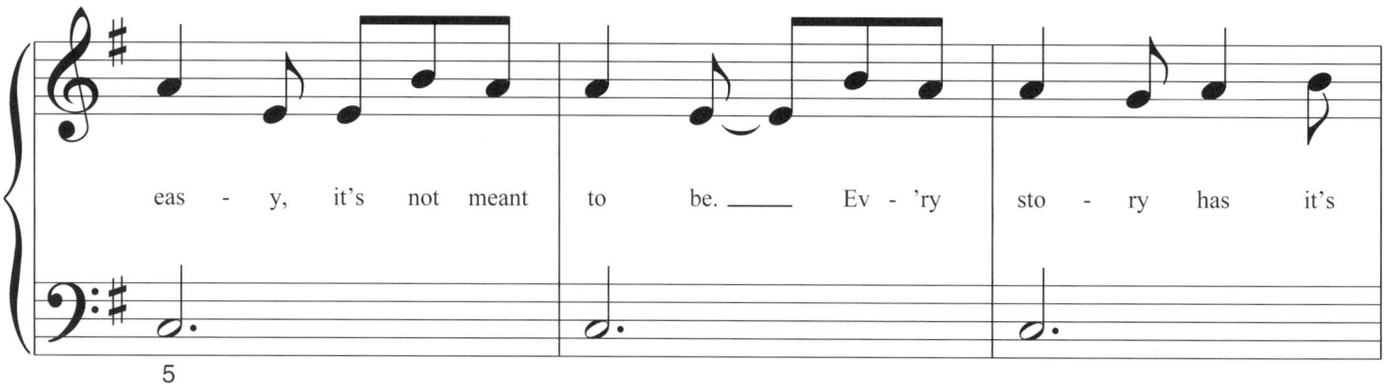
eas - y, it's not meant to be. Ev - 'ry sto - ry has it's

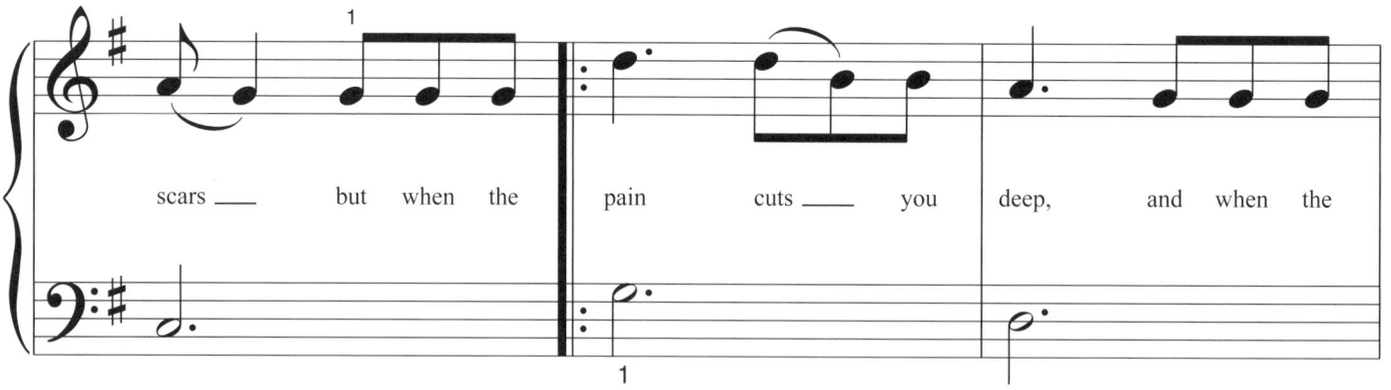
scars but when the pain cuts you deep, and when the

night keeps you from sleep - ing, just look and you will see that I will

be your rem - e - dy. When the world seems so cruel and your

heart makes you feel like a fool, I prom - ise you will

see that I will be, I will be your rem - e - dy.

1.
2.
When the

SET FIRE TO THE RAIN

Words and Music by ADELE ADKINS
and FRASER SMITH

Copyright © 2010, 2011 MELTED STONE PUBLISHING LTD. and CHRYSALIS MUSIC LTD.
This arrangement Copyright © 2016 MELTED STONE PUBLISHING LTD. and CHRYSALIS MUSIC LTD.
All Rights for MELTED STONE PUBLISHING LTD. in the U.S. and Canada Controlled and Administered by UNIVERSAL - SONGS OF POLYGRAM INTERNATIONAL, INC.
All Rights for CHRYSALIS MUSIC LTD. Administered by BMG RIGHTS MANAGEMENT (US) LLC
All Rights Reserved Used by Permission

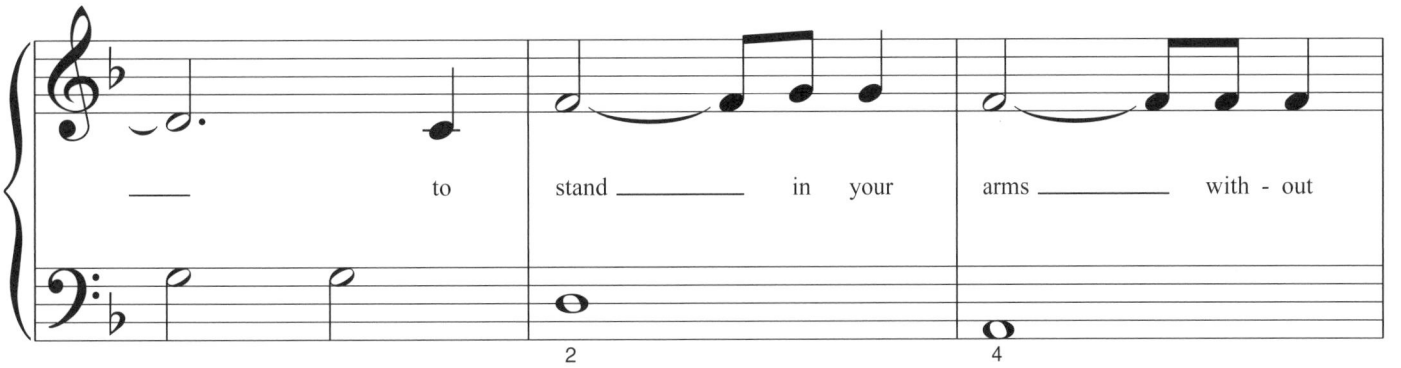
to
stand in your
arms with - out
2
4

fall - ing to your feet.
But there's a
side to you that I
2

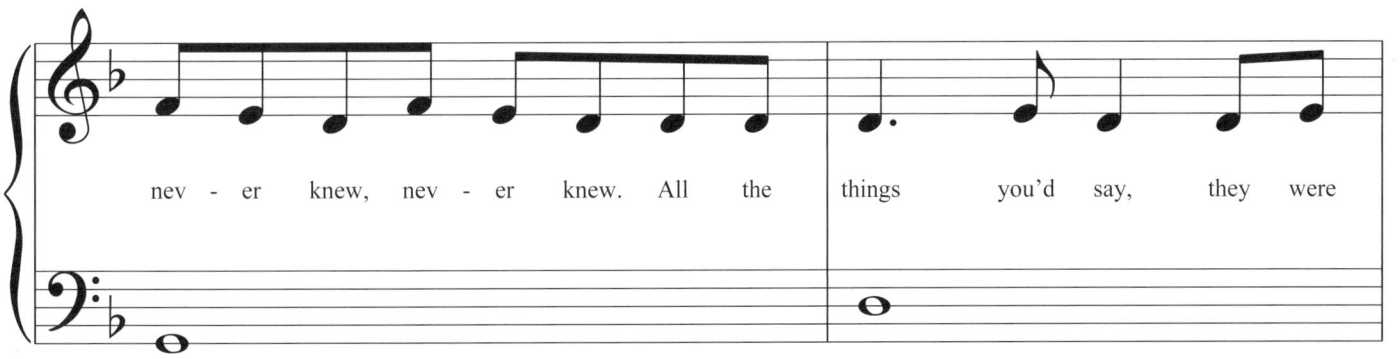
nev - er knew, nev - er knew. All the
things you'd say, they were

nev - er true, nev - er true. And the
games you'd play, you would

1
al - ways win, al - ways win.
But I set

fire to the rain, watched it pour as I touched your face.

5
Well, it burned while I cried, 'cause I heard

it scream-ing out your name, your name.
I set

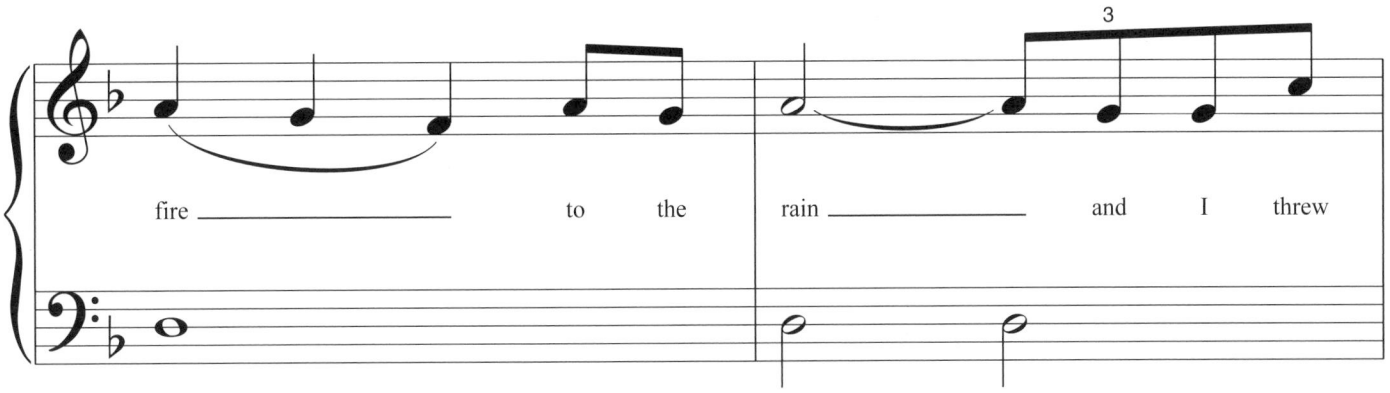
3
fire to the rain and I threw

3
2
5
us in - to the flames. Well, I felt

To Coda

some - thing die, 'cause I knew that that was the last

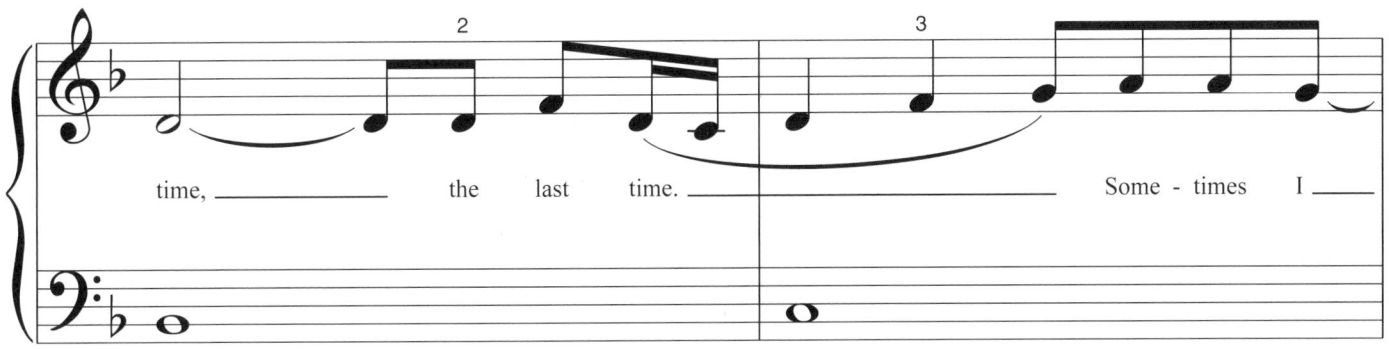
2
3
time, the last time. Some - times I

2 1 2
wake up by the door. That heart you caught must be wait - ing

for her. E - ven now, when we're al - read - y o - ver, I can't

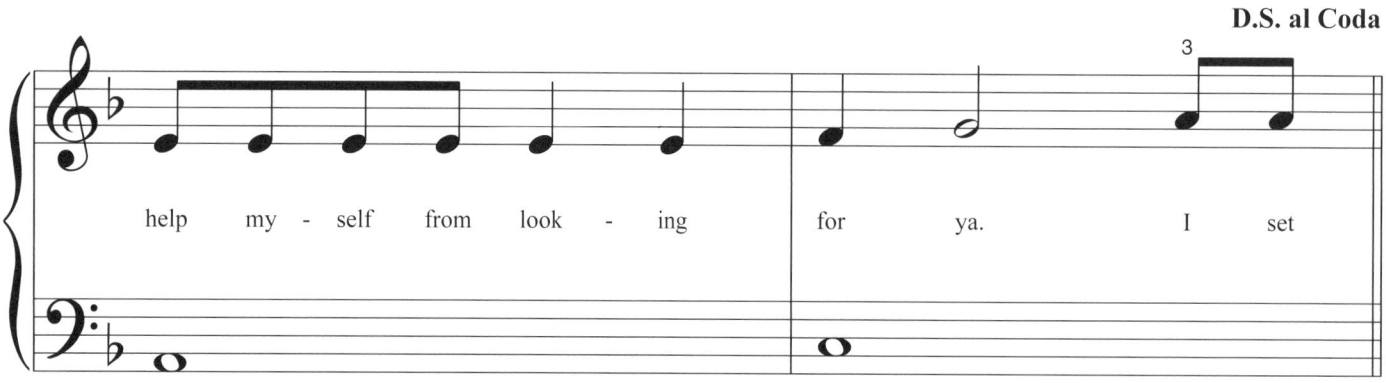
D.S. al Coda
3
help my - self from look - ing for ya. I set

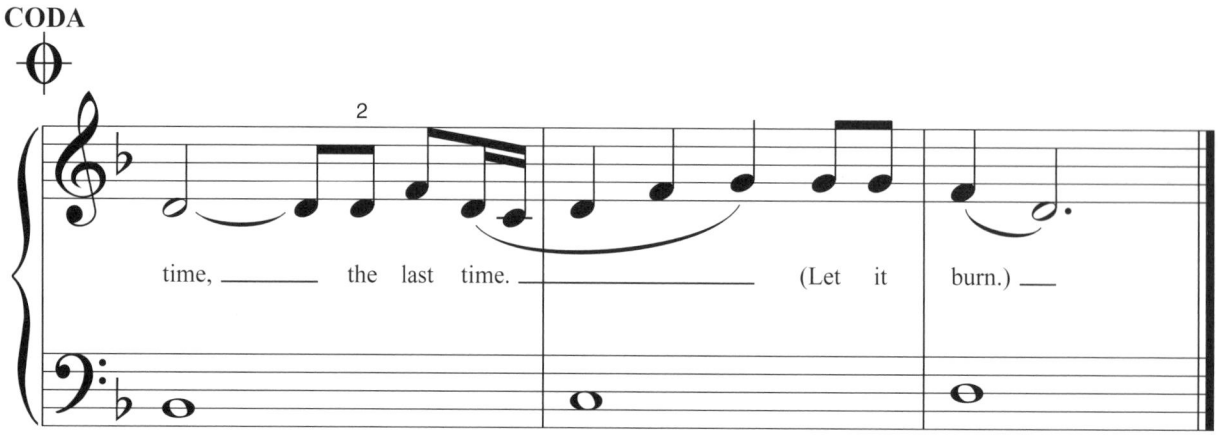
CODA
2
time, the last time. (Let it burn.)

SKYFALL

from the Motion Picture SKYFALL

Words and Music by ADELE ADKINS
and PAUL EPWORTH

Copyright © 2012 MELTED STONE PUBLISHING LTD. and EMI MUSIC PUBLISHING LTD.
This arrangement Copyright © 2016 MELTED STONE PUBLISHING LTD. and EMI MUSIC PUBLISHING LTD.
All Rights for MELTED STONE PUBLISHING LTD. in the U.S. and Canada Controlled and Administered by UNIVERSAL - SONGS OF POLYGRAM INTERNATIONAL, INC.
All Rights for EMI MUSIC PUBLISHING LTD. Administered by SONY/ATV MUSIC PUBLISHING LLC, 424 Church Street, Suite 1200, Nashville, TN 37219
All Rights Reserved Used by Permission

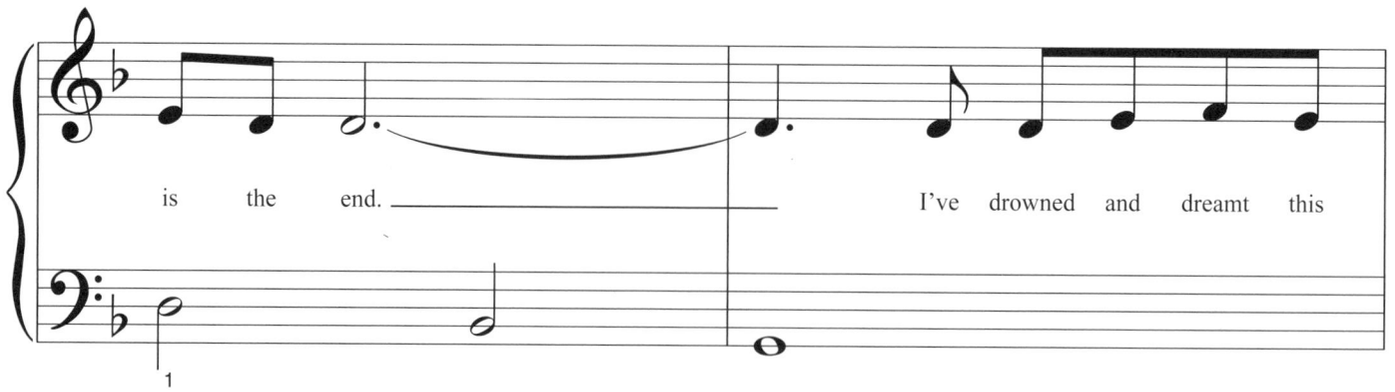
is the end.
I've drowned and dreamt this
1

mo - ment.
So o - ver - due I owe them.

Swept a - way, I'm sto - len. Let the
1
4

sky fall. When it crum - bles, we will stand tall, face it
5
5
2
1

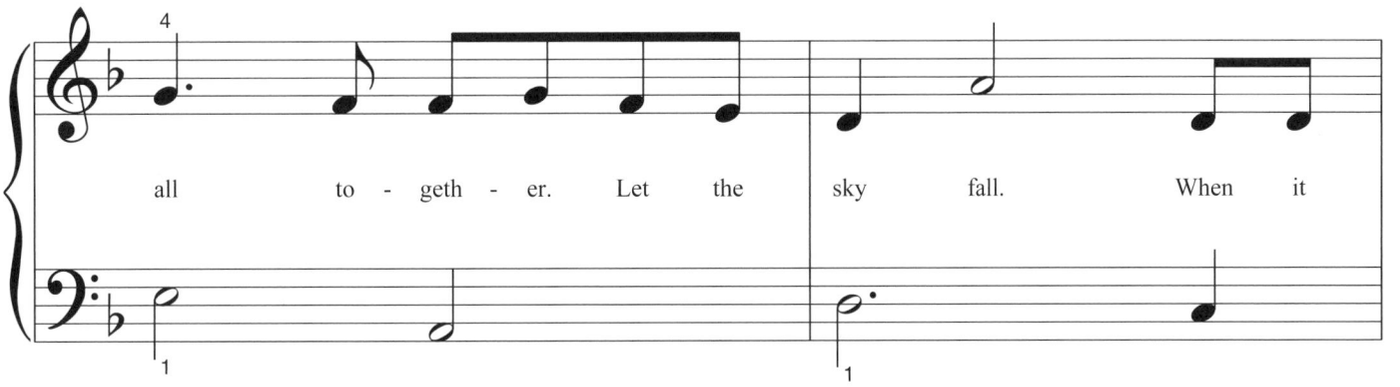
all to - geth - er. Let the sky fall. When it

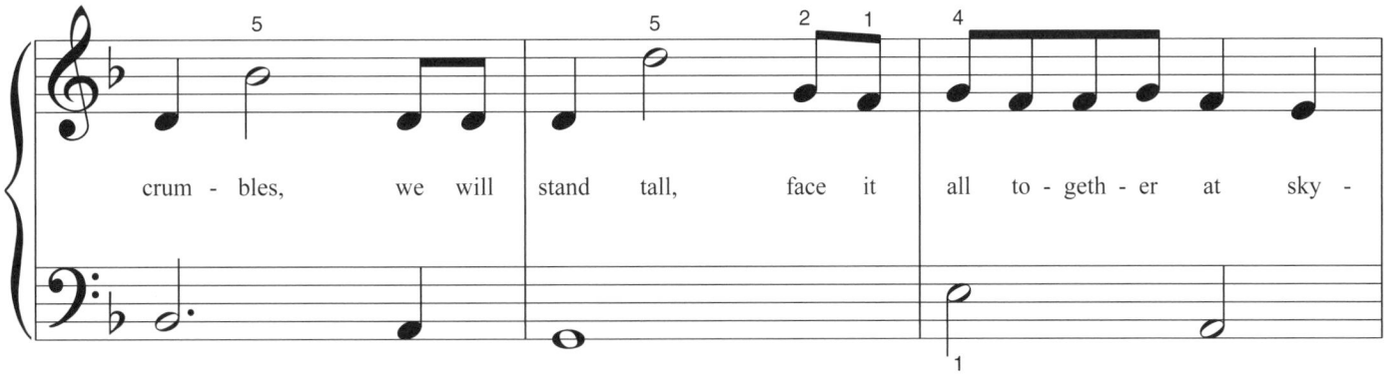
crum - bles, we will stand tall, face it all to - geth - er at sky -

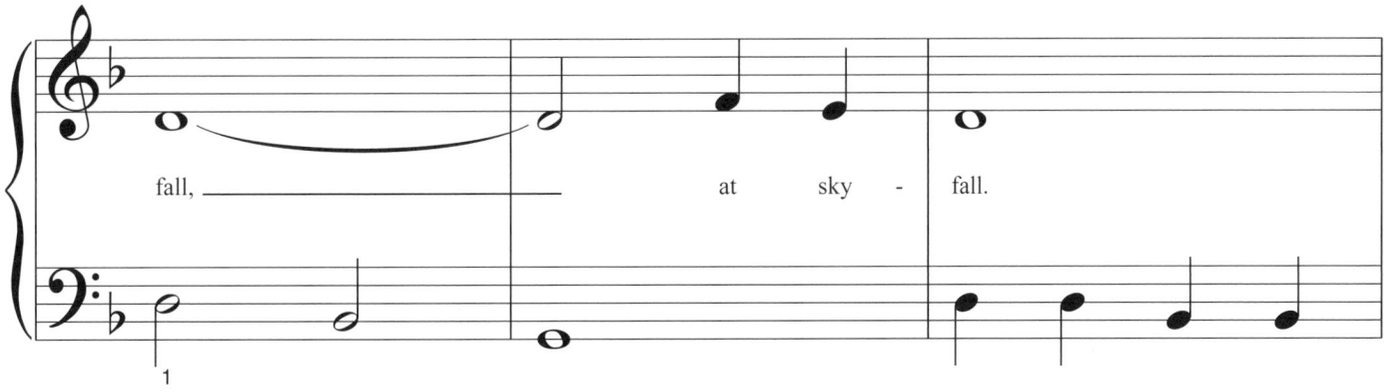
fall, at sky - fall.

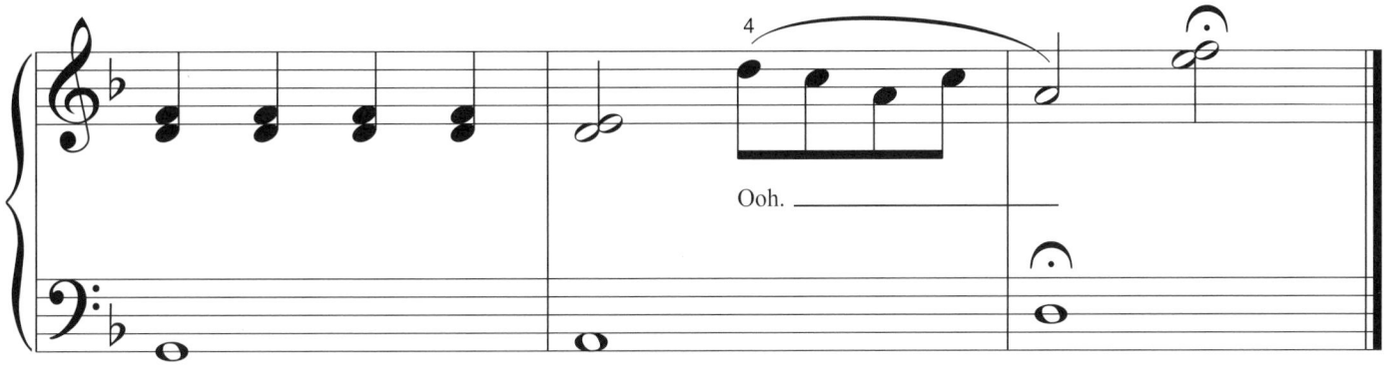
Ooh.

TURNING TABLES

Words and Music by ADELE ADKINS
and RYAN TEDDER

Copyright © 2011 MELTED STONE PUBLISHING LTD. and WRITE 2 LIVE PUBLISHING
This arrangement Copyright © 2016 MELTED STONE PUBLISHING LTD. and WRITE 2 LIVE PUBLISHING
All Rights for MELTED STONE PUBLISHING LTD. in the U.S. and Canada Controlled and Administered by UNIVERSAL - SONGS OF POLYGRAM INTERNATIONAL, INC.
All Rights for WRITE 2 LIVE PUBLISHING Administered by KOBALT MUSIC PUBLISHING AMERICA, INC.
All Rights Reserved Used by Permission

I say, ___ you al - ways say more. ___ I can't keep ___ up with your

1
turn - ing ta - bles; un - der your thumb, I can't breathe. So

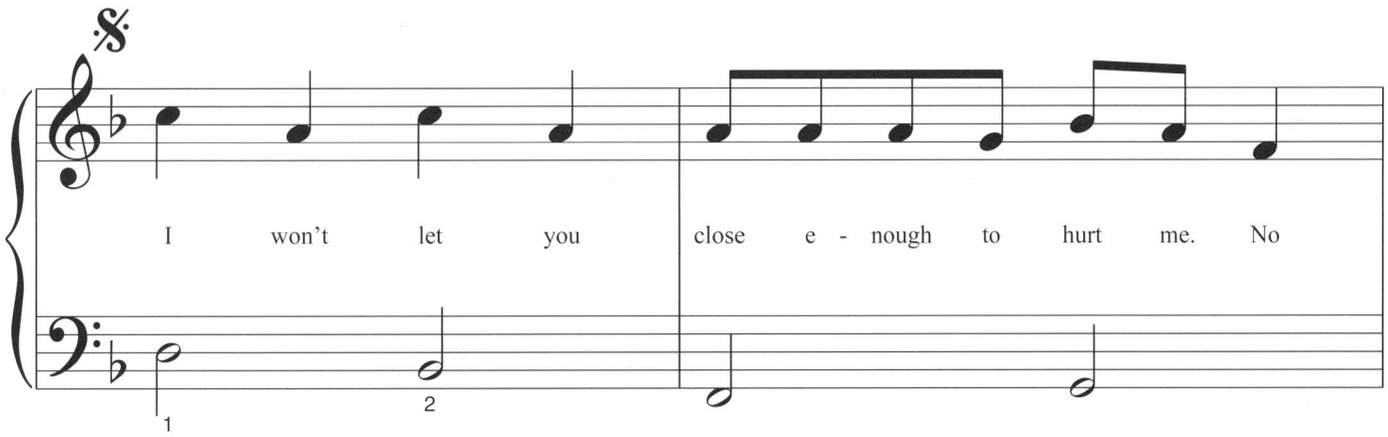
I won't let you close e - nough to hurt me. No
1
2

I won't res - cue you to just de - sert me. I can't
1
2

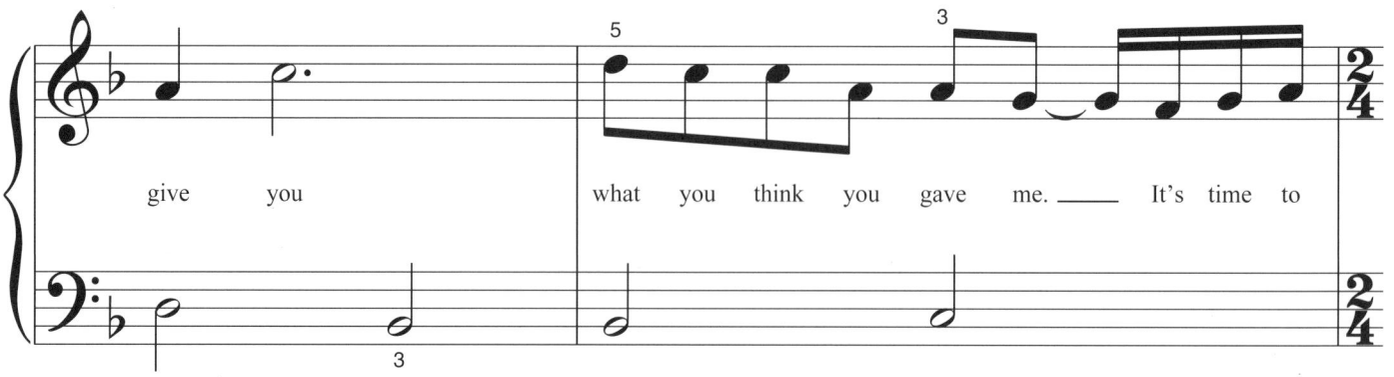
5
3
give you
what you think you gave me. It's time to
3

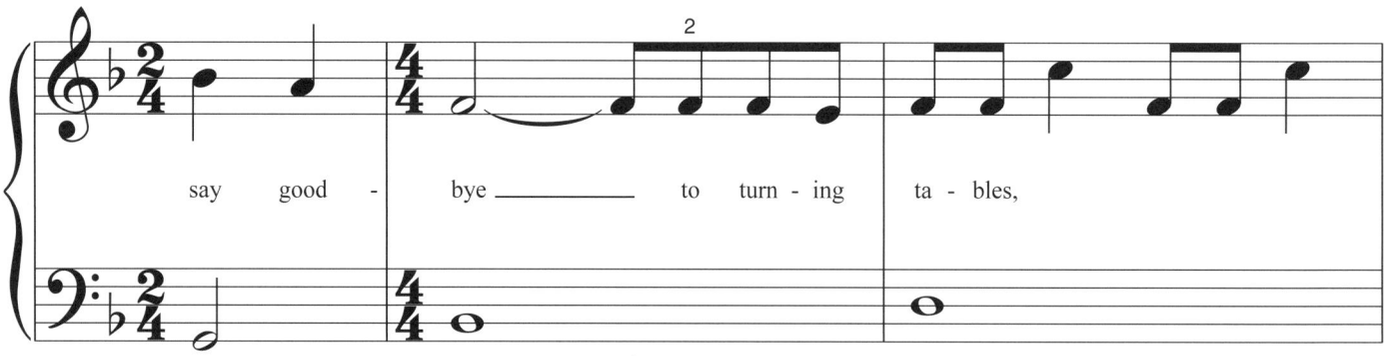
2
say good - bye to turn - ing ta - bles,

2
to turn - ing ta - bles.

To Coda
3
Next time, I'll be brav - er, I'll be my own sav - ior
1

when the thun - der calls for me.
Next time, I'll ___ be brav - er,

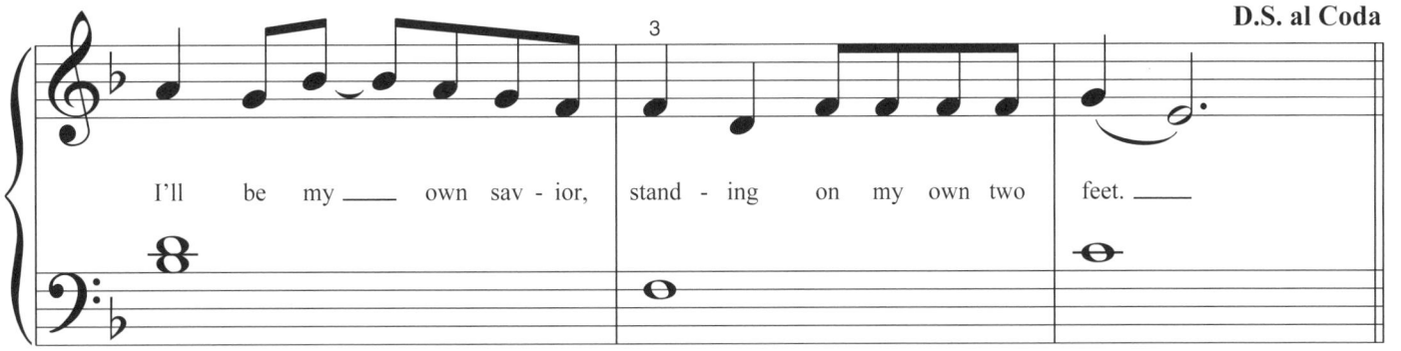
D.S. al Coda
3
I'll be my ___ own sav - ior, stand - ing on my own two feet. ___

CODA

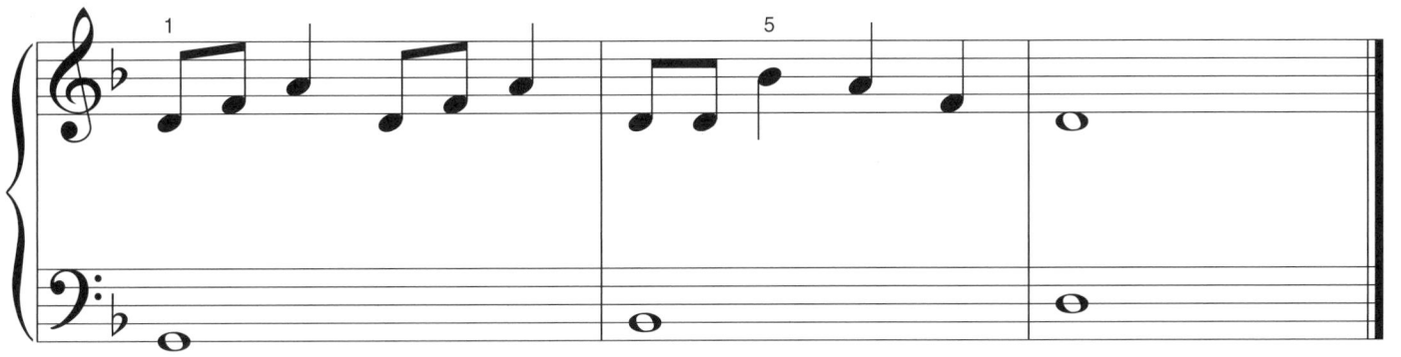
1
5

WHEN WE WERE YOUNG

Words and Music by ADELE ADKINS
and TOBIAS JESSO JR.

Copyright © 2015 MELTED STONE PUBLISHING LTD. and TOBIAS JESSO, JR.
This arrangement Copyright © 2016 MELTED STONE PUBLISHING LTD. and TOBIAS JESSO, JR.
All Rights for MELTED STONE PUBLISHING LTD. in the U.S. and Canada Administered by UNIVERSAL - SONGS OF POLYGRAM INTERNATIONAL, INC.
All Rights for TOBIAS JESSO, JR. Administered by SONGS OF UNIVERSAL, INC.
All Rights Reserved Used by Permission

But if by chance you're here a - lone, can I have a

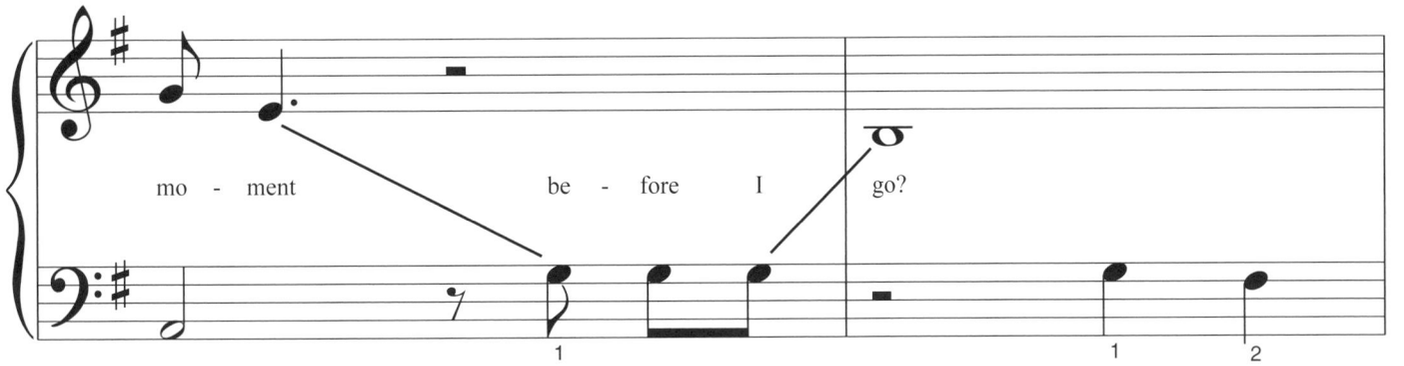
mo - ment be - fore I go?
1
1
2

3
'Cause I've been by my - self all night long, hop - ing you're
1

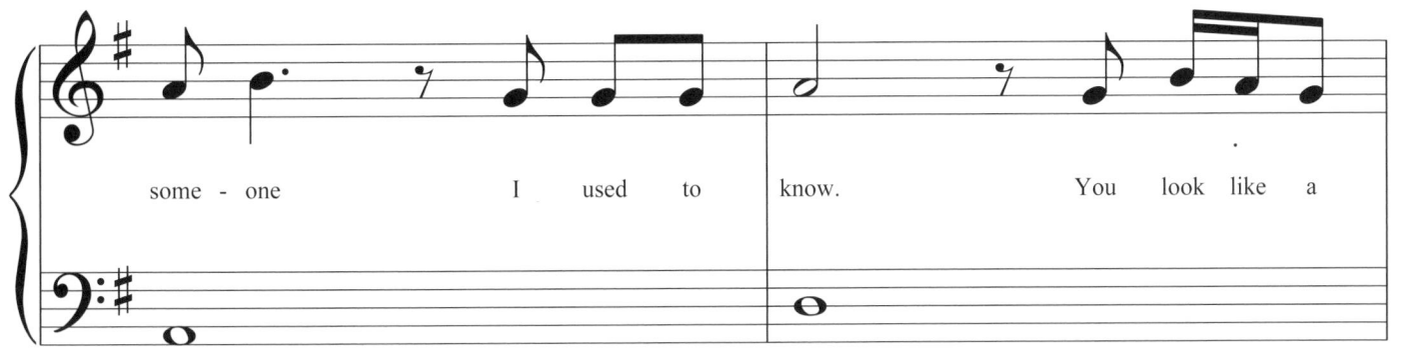
some - one I used to know. You look like a

1
5
mov - ie, you sound like a song; my God, this re -

5
minds me of when we were young. Let me
mf

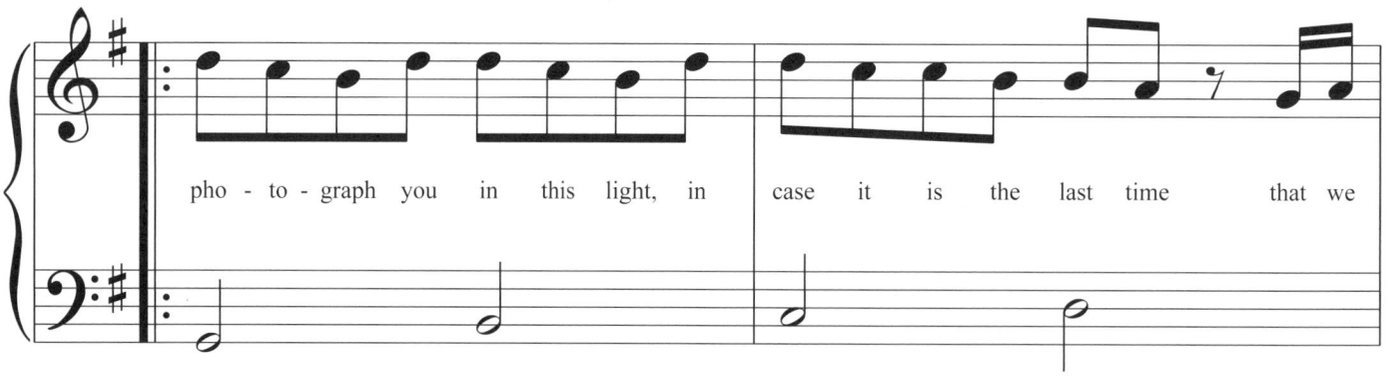
pho - to - graph you in this light, in case it is the last time that we

might be ex - act - ly like we were be - fore we re - al - ized we were

sad of get - ting old, it made us rest - less. It was just like a
mov - ie, it was just like a
1.
song. When
we were young, when we were young, when we were young, when we
were young. Let me
2.
song when we were young.

SOMEONE LIKE YOU

Words and Music by ADELE ADKINS
and DAN WILSON

Copyright © 2011 MELTED STONE PUBLISHING LTD., BMG MONARCH and SUGAR LAKE MUSIC
This arrangement Copyright © 2016 MELTED STONE PUBLISHING LTD., BMG MONARCH and SUGAR LAKE MUSIC
All Rights for MELTED STONE PUBLISHING LTD. in the U.S. and Canada Controlled and Administered by UNIVERSAL - SONGS OF POLYGRAM INTERNATIONAL, INC.
All Rights for BMG MONARCH and SUGAR LAKE MUSIC Administered by BMG RIGHTS MANAGEMENT (US) LLC
All Rights Reserved Used by Permission

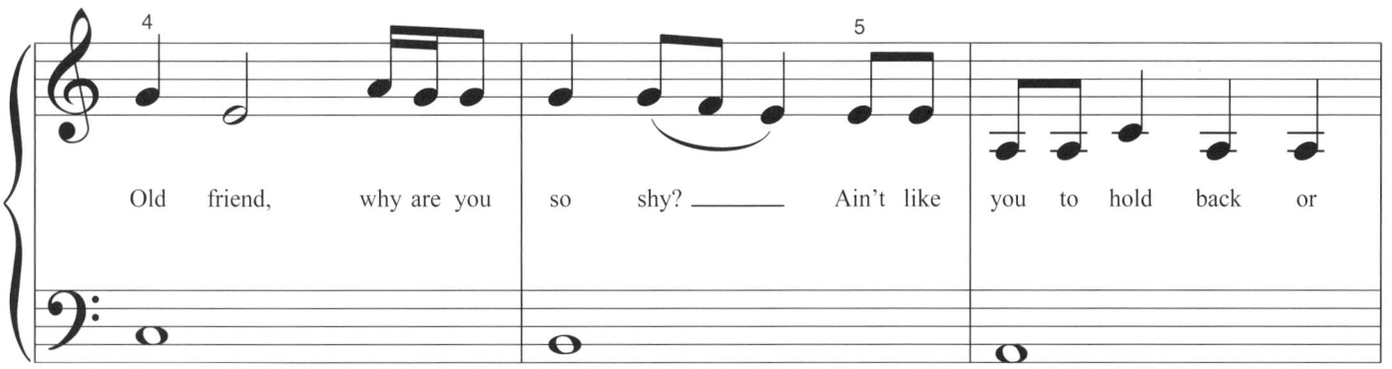
4
5
Old friend, why are you so shy? Ain't like you to hold back or

3
hide from the light.

Nev - er mind, I'll find some - one like you. I wish

3
5
noth - ing but the best for ___ you, too. Don't for - get me, I beg. I re -
mem - ber you said, ___ "Some-times it lasts in love, but some-times it hurts in -
4
5
stead." Some-times it lasts in love, but some-times it hurts in - stead.
1 3
1 3
1
2